WHITE
CRANE
SPREADS
WINGS

WHITE CRANE SPREADS WINGS

GARY HYLAND

COTEAU BOOKS

Edited by Geoffrey Ursell.
Cover painting, by Miranda Jones, "Dance of the Great White
    Bird," 1993.
Cover design by Dik Campbell.
Book design and typesetting by Ruth Linka.
Printed and bound in Canada.

The publisher gratefully acknowledges the financial assistance of the Saskatchewan Arts Board, the Canada Council, the Department of Canadian Heritage, and the City of Regina Arts Commission.

The author wishes to thank Miranda Jones for the cover art, Geoffrey Ursell for his wise editing, and The Poets Combine (Byrna Barclay, Robert Currie, Judith Krause, Bruce Rice and Paul Wilson) for their valuable input and encouragement.

Canadian Cataloguing in Publication Data

Hyland, Gary, 1940–
    White crane spreads wings

    Poems.
    ISBN 1-55050-106-2

I. Title.

PS8565.Y53W44 1996   C811'.54   C96-920063-3
PR9199.3.H95W44 1996

COTEAU BOOKS
401 - 2206 Dewdney Ave.
Regina, SK Canada
S4R 1H3

For Sharon
Again. Always.

Contents

IV

RIVER OF LIGHT

V

RECITIN FROM A FEELIN

All things work together.
I have watched them reverting,
And have seen how they flourish
And return again, each to its roots.
This I say is the stillness,
Retreat to one's roots...

–Lao-tzu

I

White Crane Spreads Wings

Courage is the price that Life exacts for granting peace.
– Amelia Earhart

The gentle flowing river
Conceals great power.
An eddy swallows
Rocks and drives a waterfall
Into deepest hollows.
Water overcomes all.

–anonymous Chinese song

A Winter Already Past

Snow is a flower without fragrance
on lower slopes by late November,
lace on the sleeves of cryptomeria,
later sifting under eaves and wooden
shutters to fringe the paper windows.
One windless night snow falls in moon-
light to quilt the trees, the forest floor,
the stacks of wood by the forester's
door. Outside he feels the cool silence
rush like the soothing tunes of flutes.

In the far shimmer a silhouette looms
and becomes a woman gliding softly,
footprints like breath on snow.
Closer, she bows in shadows, lifts
her head in light from the open door.
Such beauty he has never seen. Eyes
large, dark, glisten like winter ponds
in the pale sheen of cheeks. Features
fine as the trail of a lash from a brush
that grazes precious Kurodani paper.

When speech returns he invites her
inside. Bowing apologies she reveals
she is Shiratae from Shiranuka,
lost in dark and feather fall, seeking
the house of her grandmother Aratae.
He even finds her weeping fair when
he informs her Aratae has died. He
eases her grief, feeds and lodges her
and within a week they sleep together,
orphan woman and lone woodsman.

Bliss through winter's nine stages
whisks them to the month of melting.
One day, the woodsman wakes to see
Shiratae, in her white kimono, leaping
barefoot on the last reach of snow.
She stumbles and her robe slides down.
Running he sees only whiteness
where her skin dissolves in snow.
When he arrives the silk robe alone
remains. Beneath, a frail white flower.

Snow is a flower without fragrance
in the mountains of Himuro where
a woodsman awaits a winter already
past. He makes paper. He grinds inks
from the bark of beech and arbutus,
from chestnut husks, sapan roots,
inner skin of cinnamon, blossoms
of cherry, mountain-laquer leaves,
shoots of mugwort, sage, and holly,
and fruit of the sacred *sakaki*.

White swirls on turquoise and indigo
paper, poems for Shiratae to read,
nine each winter. Offered to the sun
in spring, his brush strokes lift like
butterflies, winking into clouds that
hang among the jagged peaks. Mixed
with wind and silences of sky, they
fall in syllables on the trees of Himuro
and whisper at the window of a sleeper
who dreams frail white flowers in the snow.

Lian Lian

1.

Though the sun in Sichuan province
has been thin with fire smoke all day
Lian Lian removes her garments
leaves them in the reeds and bathes
in the Wu Jiang's warm waters.
It is her place, her time for cleansing
with palm oil soap wrapped in cotton.
She stays out of the current's grip,
keeps her legs bent to submerge
her breasts, her shoulders, her neck,
scans the land for the hats of men.

It is now a ritual, the way she rubs
her skin red especially between
her legs, then swims back and forth
stopping often to listen for
herdsmen and the thudding water
buffalo of the sugar beet farmers.

Lian Lian slithers from the water
up the slope of long marsh grass
surrounded by bushes and beside
her garments soon falls asleep.
Later, she could not recall if she
dreamed again of the brick plant men
their calloused hands, the pain.

2.

She told the gawking doctors she awoke
in a haze, wanting but unable to turn
on her side. She was held firmly from
knees to stomach by the python's fat coils
thicker than her thighs, the beautiful
gold-black-silver design winding away
like a great banyan root down the bank.
Water droplets gleaming on its scales.

The amber-eyed snout shoots from beneath her
ribs and across her chest snaring one arm.
She feels her legs and hips being crushed.
She can manage only quick, shallow breaths.
She opens her mouth wide to risk a scream
but when the glistening head slides over her
shoulder, the wet black tongue flicking against
her cheek, without thinking, she bends forward
and bites down deep and hard just behind an eye.

She tears through the scales, rips away
a piece of flesh, moist and cold and tasting
like green bark. She spits it out. Then her head
spins and a long darkness falls upon her.

3.

Her bruised flesh as vivid as the creature's
under more hands, more instruments.
No faces, just voices – father, brothers,
nurses. A mist of whispers:

Swimming alone
              What man will
                            Wrong
Not a snake
              People are saying
                            Wrong
Demon lover
              Perhaps die
                            Wrong
No man will ever
              Deserves
                            Wrong

Day four she starts to moult. They pull silken
husks of skin, one a buttock perfectly
curved. Her hand hanging gossamer from
the nurse's hand. During the third, the last
moult Lian Lian, her fever gone, eyes open,
does not speak but sings, in throaty wobble,
love songs to the serpent.

                    The science men
are confounded and begin again to test.
Why has the fearful girl become so sunny?
Instruments once more, tubes and samples.
Once more the latex hands. Though now Lian
Lian smiles, knowing they will never know.

White Crane Spreads Wings:
The Tai Chi Chuan of Mei-lan Li

1. Maiden peers down path

Her friend San-feng says *Tai Chi*
Chuan with Master Zhao is the way
to undo your squeezing stomach
and feel calm like lakes in summer.
Mei-lan, you are too full of trouble.
No good to look at soaps all day.
You must come to sifu Zhao.
And Mei-lan whispers that she might.

2. Small child bends to story

Her mother told Mei-lan and now
she tells her only daughter Min
the tale Akeji, the merchant from Japan,
told their family long before the war.

"Woman in Night River" explains
the weeping woman sounds children
sometimes think they hear at night.

Travellers near a busy river crossing
hear nearby sounds of a woman crying…

3. Woman leans on table

Mei-lan Li's shoulders tremble
as she swallows her sobs, not to disturb
Cheng-fu and Min. When she places
her head on her arms she winces
from the welt near her eye.

But she will go with San to Master Zhao.
It is not *wu*, not combat. He need not fear.
She wants to breathe the peace.

4. Master bows, students bow

First awaken the body. This is
Pick Up Mountain. Inhale – arms
arc up and, exhale, down. This
is Golden Fountain. Right palm
centred on tan tien. Keep
spine straight so shen flows up.
Next: Shooting Bow at Eagle–
inhale aiming, exhale after.
Now Shaking Head and Tail
Removes Fire From the Heart.
Next: Make Mad Eyes at Fists.

5. Woman weeps at ford

Each night in haze of river breath
half-submerged among the rushes
she weeps for strangers to hold her child
so she may have small relief, some sleep.
Travellers approach, see no one, though
their reaching hands receive a bundle.
But when cradled, the child wails
half-choking, in dark silken layers
and she sweeps it back from sight,
and the travellers haste away.

6. Merchant makes mad eyes

Cheng-fu demands where she has been,
seizes her arm, draws her face to his,
You think Tai Chi can overpower me?
Mei-lan shakes her head, looks down.
His nails bite into her. His laughter
full of liquor. *Go to the stupid classes,*
stupid little shaking bird. Next day,
each arm has an arc of finger bruises.

7. Woman holds single whip

Stop says Master Zhao and he
comes round to inspect stances
while they hold the Single Whip.
When he reaches Mei-lan he sees
the tremor in her hands, asks
if she is cold. Mei-lan shakes her head.
When he adjusts her pose,
his hands warm hers. She trembles
more. He whispers, Your *chi*
is choked in a thousand knots.

8. Sad woman holds child

Tales of the mysterious woman reach
famous palace warrior Ju-pai Chu.
One night in breast and leg plates,
with sabres, with spears, he rides
to the ford, hears the woman weeping.
"I have journeyed many leagues. Please
hold my child that I may sleep a while."
As soon as Ju has the child and hears
its muffled cries, he gallops away,
a voice behind shrieking like a demon.

9. Man grasps lotus

At Tran's, Cheng boasts that Mei-lan obeys
without a whimper like an old country wife.
The elders nod endorsement; the young study
their cards. Home, he lies about his losses,
accuses her of stealing from the house account.
When Mei-lan offers the budget book,
he flings it down. One hand clasps his buckle.
He stands scowling while Mei-lan shudders.
Then he laughs and hauls her against his body.

10. River breaks mountain

Master Zhao shows one by one
Mei-lan and the others how to push
and gather breath, how to make
all motions a simple single grace,
a river rising from wave to wave
that never breaks. *Nothing stays
the river, not even the mountain
it erases with soft embrace.*
They learn not to do Tai Chi,
but to let each move enact itself
as the breath of mind propels.

11. Soldier unwraps parcel

Mei-lan is surprised to hear herself
revising Akeji's story as she speaks.

*Ju-pai speeds to the palace to strut
his prize before the nation's nobles
assembled by rumours of his quest.
They swarm forward when he sets
the bundle on the banquet table.
He keeps his movements slow and
long to stretch the time he has their
eyes and so make greater the surprise.*

12. Maiden sidesteps snake

When she leaves Min's room Cheng is there,
tapping his palm with her favourite figurine.
He wants her to account for the missing
minutes that made her arrive from class
at nine forty-two instead of nine fifteen.
She explains that she and San had to repeat
some figures for Master Yang. Cheng nods,
slowly replaces the figurine on the table.
Later, Mei-lan is amazed that under his sneer,
his hard-faced menace, she did not tremble.

13. White crane spreads wings

Left leg pivots left on ball
of foot. Lower left palm near
left hip as right foot follows
round and right arm rises
from waist to above right brow.

Mei-lan first feels the lightness
lift her during the White Crane,
moving from deep in waist up
to the roof of her skull, and yet
her legs and feet seem as one
through wooden floor with earth.
The lightness tickles through her scalp,
her hair. She cannot contain a smile.

14. Leaf drops in garden

When Min's eyelids close, Mei-lan stops.
Then Min's eyes open wider than before.

Silence now as Ju unwinds the silks,
one by one, layer on layer unswathed.
Between two folds, a few faded leaves
fall out, and with each unwinding more
and more flutter to the white stone floor,
cascading like an orchard in October.

15. White crane flies to nest

More careful now despite her joy
Mei-lan annoys San and declines
after class practice. Departing,
she thinks she sees a white moon blur
through the leaves – Cheng's Mercedes.

16. Embrace tiger, return to mountain

Mei-lan's feet, hips, hands move
in concert to music that sounds
like light through icicles in caves.
Her knees bend on their own, her
back stays straight and supple.
Her fingers spread and glide
as if around an unseen sphere.
Her mind conducts and yet
more and more soars free.
It rides her motions the way ravens
ply heaves of valley heat.

17. Leaves descend to rain

Someone laughed. Who laughed?
Ju turns, his forehead wet.
Silence. His hands tremble,
bump each other reaching.
More layers and more
leaves. In a fever now, Ju
feels wildly for the child. Grey,
beige, dull yellow, brittle leaves
drizzle through his fingers.

18. Young girl searches clouds

Mei-lan asks Min if she went for a ride with her father.
Min says no, she was bad, could not leave her room,
had turned her game on without permission.

Min alone. How long had Cheng lurked outside?
She must ask if Min can go with her.

Cheng says *Who cares?* Pleased she has a chaperone.

19. Waving hands in clouds

While her hands float and glide
Mei-lan imagines Ju-pai's plight,
victim of swagger and sword,
much-admired master warrior
suddenly by a woman's spell,
before his comrades, the fool.

The others turn. The music
of their movements broken
by an eruption of giggles.

20. Lifting hands to trees

More than Min, Mei-lan needs
the story now, enjoys making it
stronger. Min smiles to see
how much her mother smiles.

Ju-pai at last clutches the heart
of the bundle – a thicker twist
of leaves. Nothing but leaves,
no flesh, no life, no child to lift
in triumph. His ears burn with
smirking laughter. He roars
a wild elephant's gust of anger.
Leaves the colour of dusk, of old
men's hands, of dried blood,
cover the silver toes of his boots.

21. Young girl looks to sky

Min colours in a corner of the gym
making leaf pictures, looks up startled
when someone laughs out loud – her mother!

22. Golden cock stands on one leg

Without a wobble, she moves
on a strand of beauty,
a radiance.

This wonderful singing will
sing long and glad
its honey in her bones.

23. Riding horse to river

With taunts and laughter
swirling in his ears, Ju-pai,
his eyes red as the dragon's
remounts his still-warm steed,
and screaming
speeds to the river.

24. Waving hands in kitchen

Reaching for a cup Mei-lan's
arm moves up/down into
White Crane Spreads Wings
and the smiling soars in her.
Her breakfast waiting, she
completes the form. Min
drops her toast to watch,
afterwards applauds.

Though forbidden, she cannot
resist. Waving Hands in Clouds
is moving through her
when Cheng enters.

Her smiling stokes his rage.
He slugs her to the floor.

25. Fair lady works shuttles

Though Master Zhao has many years,
his arms, knees, hips move smooth,
low and lithe as a child's. She will
move this easy way, like water, free.

The releasing flow of chi through hands
that weave twin lines with
ease. This is the way she needs
to be. She repeats it like a plea.

26. Listens for demons

Now Ju-pai believes a demon
fox-woman lives in the river,
a weaver of illusions, clever,
with no fear of sword or spear.

Wary of serpent wiles, he
arrives to night fog, hears only
bamboo snicker, chuckle of water,
the rhythmic snigger of frogs.

27. Fair Lady hides treasure

Both palms flat on the table
Cheng hunches his shoulders,
and in his most venomous hiss
forbids any further classes.

Mei-lan pretends her old self,
glances silent down, doesn't
mention Zhao has announced
that a single lesson remains.

28. Repulse the monkey

Striding backwards one advances.
The illusion of submission
invoking the foe's assurance.

Practice please always this way
for good health and peaceful path.
Then you will have the gift of gifts.

Master Zhao and students, facing
each other for the last time, bow.

29. Searching bushes

Min wriggles and squirms,
with excitement.

Cursing, sword in hand,
Ju-pai crashes through the rushes
slashing left and right.

Fox-woman must be found,
must pay for his terrible shame.

30. Fair lady in storm

This is the most severe beating.
With Min locked screaming in her room,
he punches Mei-lan's face, rips her hair,
kicks her under the table.

Broken nose, broken ribs, bruises,
abrasions, finger burns on her throat.
A gash where the figurine shattered on her thigh.
Try your crazy dancing now, he snarls.

31. Bend bow and shoot tiger

Breath wheezes in her packed nose,
stitches and bandages bind,
body flames with pain,
but Mei-lan will do the form.
Not correctly but somehow.
Wincing, lurching, slowly
she drags through most of it
before the astonished San-feng
arrives, forces her back to bed.
Enough medicine for today.

32. Stepping into river

Min like a bird on the edge of the bed,
holding her mother's puffy hand,
protests but then agrees to hear
more of the Woman in Night River.

Ju-pai finds the very place
where he received the howling
bundle. Stabbing the darkness
he strides into a deep hole
and weighted by his armour
and the weapons he won't release,
Ju-pai bubbles to the bottom.

Min applauds. They both smile.

33. Wind opens heavy door

Twice Chen stomps through the house.
Mei and Min gone. No note. No attorney.
On the kitchen floor, the broken figurine,
chunks of glass, Mei's pink scarf, blood.
On the counter the framed family photo.
Cheng hurls it into the chandelier.

34. White crane flying

Under the willow, a waxen leaf
spirals into the circle where
Min and Mei-lan, in white
blouses billowing over red
pajama trousers and bare feet,
allow white crane wings
to lift them by feather
strokes inside their ribs.

They glide in echo of each
other in slow liquid measures
that blur like far-off voices
travelling a tranquil lake.

In violation of correct form
both are smiling.

35. Woman rests on shore

Was she a demon woman, mother?

No. Years ago she was pregnant
and died before the time, yet she
wanted so fiercely to bear her child
she would not leave with Death. So
each night she strained to deliver
her child to the living, until at last
its flesh wasted. Only crying remained.
Now she is released, now one hears
only night sounds on the river.

36. Sisters sway in garden

At last the child without a birth
dies and rides into peace. To praise
her deliverance, her sisters
dance together through the leaves.

The Head of Thomas More

After the blade's neat bite
it spun once spraying blood
and bounced inside the basket.

Spiked on London bridge
it was a hive for flies
till his daughter saved it,

bathed it and placed it
in a spice-crammed pot
she kept beneath her bed.

There the brain which had
bemused Erasmus and
fired Henry's ire

shrivelled to a rattle
behind the dreadful grin.

Public Square, Buenos Aires

Plácida Armenta shuffles in noon sun
so hot today that flies refuse to buzz.
In the plastic card on the leather thong
around her neck is her grandson's photo–
Cristo, handsome, short-haired, waiter,
the kind noticed for his grace and charm.
Beyond her, on old stones, other women walk
in Sunday clothes, white veils, sadness,
on each a necklace of grief, someone who
never arrived somewhere.

Plácida's dark eyes burn in trenches,
her nose is straight, her lips fine and thin.
Each day she sweats in this procession
around the fountain that no longer works
scorning the barred windows behind which
(beneath a fan) uniformed men sip iced tea
and compile official lists of names.

Danica at the Goya Exhibition
for Elly Danica

1.

Doctor Arrieta worked wonders and Goya lived
several more years. Your first doctor is your father
when you are four playing his special secret game
between your legs. There on the floor you want to die.
At the end of the street the moon is so full and huge
walking into it would be how you could escape
from his demands, his probing hands. Dream
of the moon, dream of being free and clean
on the dark side where he will never see, safe
in a cool moondust place. Beyond his camera's greed
for your body. What does he do with the pictures of you,
"the examinations" legs spread, or bending over his bench?

The well-bred illuminati of Madrid affecting French sniffed
at Goya's absence of poise, his violations of decorum.
Your mother, your sisters, your aunt believing you
a born carnal psychopath, lying slut, head full
of sick black clouds of vampires, witches, demons.
Salve regina, mater misericordiae you sing in the choir
thinking *Virgin Mary please please deliver me from evil.*
As Sister Camellia conducts, the big black rosary
at her side clicks against itself, and her sleeves flap like bats.
Daddy his brown suit, slicked hair, his docile wife
and your brothers and sisters fill an entire pew.
The priest beams on his good parishioner, his happy brood.
Sister Camellia's black rosary clicks and clicks.
Take off your nightie. Click. Take off your panties. Click.

2.

You owe obedience to your father as we owe obedience
to our father in heaven, explains Sister Camellia.
Pater noster qui est in caelis. If he hurts you it must be
because you are bad. How does he hurt you? You cannot say.
That is darkness. In Goya's paintings how the subjects shine
amidst a great savage darkness that wants to crush them.
El Sueno de la razon produce monstrous. The sleep of reason yields

Daddy. Looking at the family of the Duke of Osuna
you wonder which of the four is the dump child. You see fear
in the eyes of the small girl holding her daddy's hand.
And you are swallowed by another nightmare. Daddy holding
your hands, his friends on top of you, their whiskey breath,
their raspy cheeks rubbing yours. You want an axe to kill with.
To wield as the Spanish partisan in *Los Mismo*
over the French soldier himself writhing on a foe
like a man on his lover. Goya etching your soul.

Sister Camellia, is that you hooded and fleeing
beneath the witches feasting on someone in the air?
The black distended air whirling and whelping demons.
What penised menace nests in the Countess Chinchon
meek and misty in her bulging white sprigged muslin?
The philanderer Manuel Gody macho in military garb,
his thighs in palomino breeches, his walking stick
hanging suggestively between. The swinishness of men.
Even Jovellanos in his gleam of sweet reason
leaning on the ornate desk in the palace of Carlos
seems melancholy beneath the anvil of the night.

3.

The small *Caprichos* etchings tell still more of evil–
whores sweeping syphilitic customers, seen as roosters
plucked featherless, from their brothel. And the artist
sleeping while bats and owls flap about his head,
evil seeking a roost while reason dreams.
Panels from the walls of purgatory.
So much evil Ruskin set them on fire.
So much evil Sister Camellia would not look at them.
Your mother would say they are not what life is like.
And your father, would he recognize his heart?

In these images you can tell Goya wanted everyone free.
Yes, you as well. Freer than doctors and lovers have made you.
Or the absolutions that bound you to submission.
Free as Goya painting blithely in France before his death,
ideals destroyed, deaf, feeble yet captured by, capturing
the pure grace and beauty of a milkmaid in Bordeaux.

For you an abandoned church in which to paint and write
your life into peace. To make something of the sewage
and the pain. To be as clean and free as you have dreamed.
To return from the art, the darkness, your own
Arrieta, knowing as he did that *no hai remedio*–
no foot crushes all the writhing demons.
It is enough to create a cave of light.
A place to hold at bay the looming dark.

II

People We Used to Be

When childhood dies, its corpses are called adults....
                                                    –Brian Aldiss

*We are all well-advised to keep on nodding terms with the people
we used to be, whether we find them attractive company or not....
We forget all too soon the things we thought we would never forget.*
                                                    –Joan Didion

Children of Drought

1.

The past seeped from Grandfather
like the teasing rains he used to curse.
His sons crimped and withered in the caustic drizzle.
Rolled his own, smoked them down to mouse turds.
Died in 1964 wearing the pocket watch
the dust had choked to death thirty years before.
Grandfather – full of the past, finally silent, like the watch.

Bad weather burning into worse.
Wind till you're mad with it scraping your face,
grabbing your ears, long stretches of land
stripped to brick the devil couldn't cultivate.

Sun scorching you an hour after dawn,
by noon fat and blinding white, or bleary
in waves of blown soil, bleeding,
bloated, shaking in the dust.

It gnaws you to bone and grinds the bone
to chalk. You reach in for consolation
for wife or kids, something soft with hope,
and dust smokes through your fingers.

In '37 there were so many grasshoppers
guzzling such a wizzly crop they had to cannibal
themselves to stay alive.

You'd walk to the outhouse with them snapping
underfoot like twigs. Got so slippery some days,
a bit of slope and you'd fall mashing them on hands and knees.
Of course you hadda take off your boots at the back step
they got so juiced.

It's like this: the woman you loved
and who loved you good and true
turns a stony back one day.
Out of nowhere whack,
a board in the face.
That's it.
And it never goes away.

2.

Grandmother dwindled into silence
one-legged, bundled in a wheelchair.
Her sons coming twice a year
to sit for half an hour
watching weather out the window.

Every year less and less in the fields,
less and less in the pantry, the barn.
Never enough for alarm, until the day
your insides are full of space.

And you are alone, the way pain takes
you away, and it's past doing anything,
and you're too whipped to curse the gales
or governments or god. Shrivelled to chaff.

Her sons out of school at twelve
to scrape for dollars, their promise
twisted on itself like Russian thistle.

Making do, pinching and scraping.
Newspaper window shades,
newspaper place mats, newspaper logs.

Sowing love in the dust,
the illusion of land above the land,
roots singed, gnarled, hard.

Married in borrowed clothes, they
honeymoon a weekend down the track.
A diamond, a house – too far down the line.

3.

Grandchildren with bottle cap and clothespin toys,
prying the outhouse door against snow,
the chimney pipe for bedroom warmth,
smashing pails through dugout ice for bath water,
hearing litanies of real deprivation
and learning frugalities of light switch and stove.

We never acquired a bounty of joy. Our scraggly
spirits content with convenience. Cramming dreams
in pockets full of holes. Flat, storm-squinted eyes.

Our thirties. And we've regressed to their
depression. Bruised by their ways, their myths.
Dreaming downpours, dreaming rainbows.

We were going somewhere. To the mountains,
to the sea, to primrose and laurel meadows,
I don't know, somewhere far, not here–
stifling in a room, dust blasting
through our lives, grit in our teeth, words
lost like straw in the wind.

And there is recourse that we refuse to seek.
And there is relief that we won't stoop to take.

The fridge expires, the Chev
wheezes and dies, the TV fails,
as we knew they would,
in the gusts that drove
the rubble through our lives.

There never was plenty.
The vans would arrive. The dust
would come and divest us.

And love – those wan daisies
Grandmother nursed one spring,
the ones the last horse ate.

November

Brittle leaves scuttering the street. Streams of chimney smoke blurring
　　into clouds.
Wind grey and sleek packing gutters with snow. Trees bleak, beyond
　　meaning now,
not manic cuneiform, not gestures of disease, not eunuchs grim
　　in the shrill light.

You lean to this. You feel knees spreading to release you. Hands that
　　clasp and knot
your bleeding. You feel your breathing begin, the vague pain
　　fibrous beneath
your scream. You see the grey radiance, the white spaces, the sheen
　　of polished steel.

You feel the topaz talisman. Its pale gleam. You receive drawings
　　of a beast, a sky,
so that you may see all that you are, all that you will be. An amber
　　fog twines along
the water where you must kneel, the river that meanders deep into
　　the hallowed land.

The river becomes a creek freezing. A forgotten tent torn, dreaming of
　　grass, dreaming
of arms, lovers humming. Shreds filling with distance and wreckage
　　of reeds.
The hermit of the sedge who would have hailed you has retreated to
　　another month.

Sleep is your response. Sleep defeats time. Until something in you
　　stretches, yawns
and conceives spring, even now, and you clamber the slopes
　　steeper and steeper
to celebrate winter's easing. The air cuts deep. You breathe keen
　　flakes of glass.

No thaw. The month moves with you, your cowl. The moon a gleam
    on the creek's
dark ice. Something wants warmth, something sings fire. You gather
    willow splinters,
the stems of rushes, leaning stalks of yellow grass. You will please
    whatever sings.

No

No, he cannot cross the bridge
to the deer pasture on the other side.
Does he want to get stomped into sausage?

No, he cannot go to the bear compound
till Daddy wakes up to be his guide.
Does he want to be clawed and eaten?

No, he cannot go to the big playground
where those bad boys are wrecking the slides.
Does he want to get bruised and beaten?

And no, no, not to the paddle boat ride,
No use to mope, no use to moan and sigh.
If he drowned, wouldn't he be sorry?

Okay, he can visit the wild bird side,
but no further than Peacock Lane,
till Mommy's through reading her story.

Pheasant and grouse walking in rings.
Then the frantic Sandhill Crane,
its head scraped in a low-roofed stall,

trying to open its huge grey wings
against one rail and one wire wall.
He's rooted there when she comes by.

No, no no, he can't stay here and cry.
He's not a girl to sniffle and bawl,
and the stupid bird will never fly.

First Death
for Doreen Bastedo

I found it in a green velvet case
in the grey light of a failing winter.

A coil of pale blonde hair.

Gathered with faded ribbon
and clipped to a letter.

A doctor writing
my aunt from the sanatorium
that my cousin was dead.

Her lungs surrendered
and someone, my mother most likely,
who would have done her hair,
saved these strands.

First death resurrected after
so many others.

Winter has been long and harsh
gouging with burrs of ice,
jagged gusts,
two more deaths.
I want it in its grave –
nothing clipped from it
nothing saved.

I want a wide-striding summer
its farthest foot in November.

I want death human,
wealthy, winter-spent
and sailing to a distant season.

Pintsch Compression Company Tour

I am ten when I follow my father along the narrow, ankle-deep rut the workmen have worn in the weeds. Over a footbridge, through the roundhouse thrumming with monstrous steam engines (greasy men in grey caps staring), down the concrete steps into the squat brick building that reeks of oil and gas. I scurry as he almost disappears in the gloom. Grime is steamed on the windows. Floor, walls, ceiling – black with soot. Dingy lamps smolder in metal cages. I am shown the storage tanks, compressor, pumps, and valves, the huge pipes that take gas through tunnels under the mainline tracks. The giant hose with metal couplings that he plugs into the cars, or the Pullmans don't work. So the fancy people can be served cornish game hens. So they can wear shirtsleeves as they tunnel through winter. He wipes a gauge with a rag, explains the range of readings, shows me the log book, the columns of smudged numbers. The punch clock and cards. Seven years, never an absent shift.

I recall picnics cancelled, ball games missed, the fringe of beer bottles around his chair. I want to be running with Tippy or drawing pictures of my secret place. No, I haven't any questions. I follow him back to the bridge, its timbers warm in the sunlight. He tells me I can make it from there.

Years later, long after the funeral, with three sons of my own, I understand and weep. Then I sit and write nine questions about compressors, gauges, trains.

Consequences

It is a summer after supper,
the stars just starting to form,
and Sharon Armour is the judge.
She has grade seven lore and we
are mere grade four or fives.

I wear the striped green T-shirt
that helps me pretend I am
a sailor on the river. Though Mrs.
Merrit's housecoat sways on
wire like a phantom chaperone,
we play Truth or Consequences.

When it's your turn you choose
to answer a question or suffer
a fate of short and long kisses
with a partner of the judge's whim,
a brief Morse Code liaison
in the garden behind Merrit's garage.
I usually prefer Truth because
we river sailors have better
wishes than rubbing lips with
Sherry Merrit or Betty Ogden.

But this one's too risky, nothing
I dare answer. I try to disguise
my pleasure when the judgement,
five short and five long, is with
the judge herself, forerunner
of the older women of my desire,
tall, brown-eyed, dark-haired
in jeans and shiny penny loafers,
new breasts like strawberries
beneath her white sweater.

We huddle in the drooping grass
on the garden's edge, kiss in slow
tremors, and talk a bit between.
The stars surge with liquid light.
After eight she asks how many
and, as coolly as I can through
the spin and daze, I answer six.
During number twelve, moister,
more sustained, I hear a voice.
Not my mother, nor my brother
sent to spy and drag me home.

It is so familiar to me now.
This night it seems more urgent
with each shout, as if the caller
wants me home because he knows
all garden myths must fall to grief.

To the Rescue

They hear my guttural snarl,
the back door bursting open–
three grade sevens on my brother
in the alley, whacking with fists
and boots. I will thrash the buggers
good, at last use the boxing moves,
the football muscles. I can see
crushed cheekbones, broken teeth–
splinters in a mash of red pulp.
They startle like buzzards disturbed
and fly up Fifth Avenue while I
pause just long enough to see
the victim's well enough to cry.

Pounding up the street and into
Empire playground, I am starting
to gain, confident in three year's
seniority on the streets, and hoping
they are too dim and fearful to see
they have the edge – my size and fury
no match for a three-on-one blitz.
I grab a shortcut through the hedge
into Welcher's field breathing so
hard I know I'll have to sit and rest
on the first catch before I murder him.
When one looks over his shoulder
I see the bright-eyed twist of fright.
Reaching Coteau Street now, less
than half a block ahead, they split,
leaping low fences and cutting
between houses. This is their patch.
I'll not catch and kill anyone here.

Back home my brother watches TV.
Because I saved his ass and he has
only cuts and bruises, I can strut
my power, lecture him again on
how to duck the eyes of bullies
and where to run when you can't.
He sits on the couch our mother
patched with old housecoat scraps
and gazes blankly out the window
while some TV cowboys chase some
other cowboys over tired-looking hills.
I might have been sentenced to hang
for dropping some snot-faced lunk
or got shellacked by their fists and boots
because my brother acts like a girl
and has no discretion and can't fight
worth a bag of shit and doesn't know
how to dodge a bunch of shitforbrains
and sits there crying just because
he got conked a few and doesn't like
being told the truth about himself.

But I don't know the truth and I won't
for three years, and when I do
it will take three more before I wouldn't
prefer the slug of fists and boots.

Northland Pro

My father said the Northland Pro was the world's finest hockey
stick. This back when I was shorter than the boards on the
outdoor rink and he was skating for the Hornets. That's when he
bought his only Northland. Mother cursed it – a sliver of wood
worth more than half a ton of coal.

He showed me how to judge the lie, the grain, the splice, the
shaft for flex and strength, how to space and roll the tape and
seal it, sizzling, on the stove. To keep the moisture out, he
varnished it, then stood it, perfect and golden, by his equipment
in the spare room. At night when he was at work, I'd creep in
and hold it, so incredibly light and balanced, smell the mix of
varnish, tape and wood and feel the hat-tricks flying from its
blade. Too beautiful to ice with the cheaper hacking sticks, the
gouging steel.

Each year, even after he'd hung up his skates and I wore them on
the high school team, he'd sip beer, add another coat of varnish
and talk to that Northland about what they could have done and
might yet do. But he got stuck on night shifts and rye and never
did see me play, even after he retired, the curved blade and
fibreglass days. When he died, the Northland passed to me. It
sits in the closet of my den, and once a winter, even now that I've
hung up the skates, I open a beer, take it out, dust the darkening
wood, and tell it what we might have done.

Our Fathers

Snow is heaved in wings along the drive,
sun a pale moon in crystal mist.
We shiver past tombstones, our boots
the first to break last night's snowfall,
comparing fathers, having agreed
he was not the same for both of us.

The razor holes in the albums
where you cut him from your side
sometimes taking parts of yourself.
You lament the cavern he made
in you, gnawing your days.

And I was alone on a windy field for years.
I don't recall him ever touching me
for anything, not even the beatings you curse.

Row after row and we cannot locate the spot
among the polished stones of finer fathers.
The cold rips into us on the wind and
upward from the permafrost of bones.

His marker is thin and black. His name, ours,
is grey. The inscription, the sole tribute
we could muster, seeming almost holy,
Dad. We brush the snow away, mutter a few
banalities. Then turn in silence for the road.

Times My Mother Wasn't Going To Die

1.

The first time she wasn't going to die
she was still spitting my cowlick down.
The house was warm with raisin pies,
and she was sprinkling cinnamon
on strips of dough to make the crunchy
cookies I loved, and talking over
her shoulder to Mrs. Boyle at the table
drinking coffee, smoking, long legs twined,
toes tucked behind an ankle. They
spoke of the afflictions of mothers
and Mom was ahead because Grandma
had a stroke and would never speak or
walk again, face forever warped. Mom
was better looking than Vera Boyle
and I was proud she was winning when
suddenly she said, *I want to die quick,*
before I become someone else's burden.
My comic book trembled at the horror
of being motherless. I crossed my fingers,
unwished her wish with my best magic.

2.

But her wishing proved stronger.
At eight what do you know of cancer?
Something your aunts whisper,
one of the bad words. A rat thing that
eats you from the inside, its snout
oozing in Gracie Smith's armpit.
On a calendar she kept the names
of customers, the shut-in, busy or
idle women who had trims or perms
in their kitchens. Dead women
the funeral homes paid for, dead
of cancer. In one square she wrote

"Operation," in thick letters
and after it nothing, blanks where
I would always be telling teachers
My mother is dead. The doctor
gave her a tonic called Odds to
help her survive but I knew better.
This would take work, weeks and weeks
of prayer so pure the saints would
pool their halos for a magic cure,
hours of dishes, dusting, sweeping,
A's in arithmetic and science,
my plates cleaned of peas, a truce
with my brother, sitting up straight,
not walking with hunched shoulders,
and no more pinching Malted Milks.
She came home looking small, pale,
and weary, but soon her calendar
refilled with customer's names.

3.

When the grade fives squirmed through
the funeral of Albert Thul's mother,
when the nuns took the grade tens
to the protestant service for Gary
Smallwood's mother, I was grateful
mine was at someone's house cutting
hair, gossiping, drinking coffee.

4.

Coffee, coffee, coffee and Black Cat
cigs and a sniff or two from a jar
of gasoline kept her sharp enough
for spats with Dad and cutting
three hundred new clients – patients
at the training school for mentally
handicapped adults, every level–
drooling mutes in diapers, thrashers

strapped in chairs, the emotionally
swindled reading Jane Austen.
The ones who apprenticed with her
came to stay weekends and holidays,
got to play bingo and shop downtown.
And Mom got cancer again, went in
Mother's Day and the next morning
had all her mother's fixtures torn out.
I kissed her, prayed and bargained
nights when God heard best, went
to church for the first time in years.
I had buddies, girlfriends, rock and roll
and a job, yet out of sight, the boy
with the comic book crossed his fingers.

5.

She returned withered, her evil cells
cremated in a bag, and I resumed
my adolescent dissipations.
The next threat was her hands, what
doom they might pour in her coffee,
blades they might plunge into her,
the knots they knew. My college
psych class insights were no comfort.
Small red capsules soothed her hands,
and electric gusts blew her nightmares
into empty fields where she was lost.
So she wandered to former gardens,
gathered iris and lilac bouquets,
and, high on the aroma, blossomed.
She rented his and hers suites
blocks apart, furnished them and told
Dad his was the third-floor dump.
The first woman in town to conduct
her own divorce, she lived on her own
six years then married a beautician.

6.

The last time I saved her life
was a hot breeze-free July night,
my sons snuggling after a dose
of *Huckleberry Finn.* I was brushing
my teeth when the phone rang.
Her husband crying, hysterical,
"She's not breathing. Your mother
collapsed. I can't ... I can't ... can't–"
I told him to call an ambulance,
grabbed a shirt, vaulted barefoot into
the car and raced the mile to save her.
No charms, no prayers, no deals for
God, spitting toothpaste, running stop
signs, reviewing first aid routines.
She was on the bed. He sat moaning
on the kitchen floor. No ambulance.
Too shocked to call. I screamed
him to the phone as I went to work,
the first time in years our mouths
had touched, her chest rising as I
coaxed her between breaths, told her
now wasn't the time, her grandsons
needed her, I needed her, I needed
her, the chest lifting, tears running
into my mouth, into her mouth. She
was going to make it. Yes. Her chest
was lifting. The medics came with
their miracle luggage and we sped
to the hospital. Everyone in white
scrambled to her room.
                    I stepped
outside to see the sky, to know
everything was in place. And it was.
A shimmer of stars through tears.
Then they told me she was dead.
A blood clot to the lung had killed
her fast. I had been inflating
her chest through shreds of tissue.

She was dead. I sat with her
a while, wept goodbye to whatever
part of her was listening and
scolded her for wanting this. I would
have preferred, I explained, to have her
old in bed, me bringing trays of food,
and coffee, some room for atonement.
But she knew better.
There would be no unwishing by
the stricken boy with the comic book.

Phantom Parents

1.

We become their ghosts.
I brush my hair, knife a letter
open, appease a telephone pest,
and my father is also there.
The way last night I guzzled coffee,
shunning sleep, straining to wrest
a figment into reality – that
was my mother. And the nuances
that merge them both, the covert
traces others notice, are there.
These words, syntax, cadences–
what flickers of them echo back
to my grandmothers' kitchens,
my grandfathers' sports and crops?
Habits, gestures, inclinations
I couldn't see I see better now
that I've grown protective lenses.

2.

Nine when her father died, mother
was never sure if what she recalled
of him was him or imagination.
After her death I find in her things
a worn pencil note from Rochester
sent a month before his heart failed.

July 2nd, 1925
My Dear Little Iris, Your kind
letter received and glad to hear
you are praying for your papa
and I know you will show Lorane
and Joseph how to say a little
short prayer for daddy to get well.
I will not forget yous at home in mine.
Your loving Daddy, Omer.
Her mother left to steer five kids
through drought and depression.

3.

My father at eight stumbling
after his father and the pointer
Rex on a partridge hunt, asked
for a drink and was told to hush.
Later he was kicked for lapping
with the dog from a weedy slough.
He recalled his father crouching
to shit by the path, gun casual
across thighs, pointed at his head.

Delivering papers at twelve
he missed death by minutes.
After a smoke behind Woolworths
on a muggy August day. He was
a block away when the brick wall
he'd leaned on exploded into
the alley. Stacks of celluloid collars
in spontaneous combustion.
Longer butt and I'da been killed,
he'd say, then cackle to himself.

4.

What calamities, cruelties,
trifles, what drizzles of habit,
chemical gluts or droughts,
whispers of myth and archetype
cut them too deeply for love?

5.

I was astonished to see,
daring the family album
after several years, so many
snaps where they seem happy
together, the last from 19
52. Fourteen years later
after barrels of pills
and the shock treatments
Mother lawyered her own divorce.

6.

Some days I would lie full-length
for hours in wheat grass and weeds,
sun warming my shirt and jeans,
waiting for one of them to leave.
I'd dream jackpots to expunge
the poverty that gouged their days,
recite lines from their songs like charms
so they could live *La Vie en Rose Under
a Blanket of Blue Over the Rainbow.*
I'd track clouds and sometimes after
a night of skirmishes, I'd sleep.

7.

After death they're perfectly
ours. As when children we were
theirs. Their last hurtful frailties
a gestation into this further birth.
And we play with them as they
played with us. I set them like dolls,
tame, embracing, finally able
to resolve the mysterious plight
that throttled their love.
To catch at last a hallway caress,
some morning tenderness, no need
for booze or furtive whiffs of gas.
The feuds they returned to like
devoted customers resolved as
I would have smoothed them
from where I trembled on the stairs.
I remember willing them to kiss
then waltz while the kitchen
shimmered with harps and violins.

MichaelMark

Your names become a collective noun – MichaelMark.
A three-year-old, a four-year-old in endless competition,
a crazy graph of making war and making up.

Each day calibrating what counts and what doesn't,
no better than the rest of us at separating the joys of triumph
and participation, but needing the other's opposition.

When you storm up in tears I explain: *Boys, you are one,*
like your hands, left and right, that can resist or assist
each other. See this hand is Mark, this Michael.
Now they push against each other and grow strong,
now they lift this chair together. That's how things get done.

Ah, sweet reason, paradigms of Logic 101 applied
to fraternal spats. In no time you are bored with wisdom
and roar away to devise another tussle, Michael yelling,
I'm the right hand. I'm the right.

Before Monitors in Nurseries

We were young and gullible and as happy
as naive near-poverty allowed. I had
been teaching for three years, and with two
degrees earned almost as much as the janitor
on my floor. We had an upstairs suite,
with a lattice gate to keep the boys from death
on the stairs. Mark, three, and Michael, two.
It was before second-hand smoke caused
cancer, so Linda puffed while prying spinach
between clenched lips. It was before
five causes of crib death, ten ways to child-
proof your kitchen, caps for electrical outlets,
and monitors in nurseries. They had yet to announce
perverts in playgrounds. The four-door Comet
had lap belts only but none in the back. When
we went driving, the rear doors were locked
and the boys rolled and romped with stuffed
bunnies and rubber airplanes on air-bubble
plastic seat covers. But who knows how one day
we forget to check the doors or chubby-fingered
Mark somehow levers up his lock. It is
a Sunday afternoon in July. As I turn on
the banked curve at the bottom of the steep
hill that enters River Park the scene throttles
to slow motion – a click from the door behind me,
instant fear in Linda's eyes, behind her Michael
in the mirror leaning left, beside him nothing
where Mark should be. My left hand is steering,
my left foot braking, my right knee against
the seat back as I twist, grope backward
and grab Mark's ankle as he slides out.
The car stalls halfway around the curve but
I have him and haul him back onto the seat.
I restart, pull over, collapse on the wheel,
shaking with fright and exhilaration.

Maybe we argued about who should have checked
the door. Maybe we laughed and went for ice cream.
That's all gone. I know that night I wept and prayed.
After the birth and the birthday parties, the swings,
the stories, the romps and rhymes, the special
rituals and the silly secret phrases, how fast
you can lose so much. So much that will be lost.

Final Measures
for Miles

This is the room where the newborn die in glass boxes. The floor is terrazzo. The walls a gaseous green. Two large windows behind yellowed venetian blinds. No pictures. No bunnies on wands. No incubators. No respirators. That was yesterday. The two hydrocephalics, the incomplete spine, the malformed heart lie under small white blankets without movement. And there is not a sound. This is the room of final measures. This is where they have placed my son.

Starving to death. His stomach sealed like a tomb. Two weeks old and looking like an old man wasted with emphysema, every bone pressing skin. The futile intravenous looping from his head.

While my wife sleeps in the lounge, I watch the priest finish the emergency baptism – some words, a dab of holy water, a sign of the cross.

Then I am at work teaching poems to adolescents. Because the contract says I can have three days only after my son dies. Because substitutes cost $90.00 a day and Jacobs the principal is stern. Because no one has ever died on me and I don't know what to do.

During lunch a meeting with the doctor and the out-of-town surgeon. My wife seems like one of the staff, serious, calm. I hold her hand while the doctor explains they now have a diagnosis and that it wasn't his fault it took six days. The stomach so distended he couldn't feel the almond-sized growth that sent the pyloric valve into permanent spasm. I imagine this man prodding my son's swollen stomach, my son's life depending on the sensitivity of those plump fingers.

The surgeon draws a diagram of what needs to be done. The incision will run from sternum to groin. And the odds, given my son's condition, are not the best, maybe one in three. Stupidly, I look at my watch. Fifteen minutes before the first afternoon class. I say *Of course, do it. What choice do we have?* My wife agrees.

Afterwards, she doesn't speak, walks the other way down the corridor, and numbly I return to work.

Just over an hour later Jacobs relieves me. Important call. It was a success, and I am released, though not into joy. No hitches for my son, but as I speed to my room, where Jacobs scowls impatiently in the door, I realize my complications have just begun.

III

Parts of Our Lives Break off

Everyone alters and is reduced by everyone else. We are all the time taking in portions of one another or else reacting against them, and by these involuntary acquisitions and repulsions modifying our natures.

–Gerald Brenan

All changes, even the most longed for, have their melancholy; for what we leave behind is part of ourselves....

–Anatole France

Vacant Afternoons

1. Present

Snugged to the earth, his open eye
sees a small stone, pink with black flecks,
the base curved like a keel casting
a pointed shadow. It rests on granules
of reddish soil, though a few in the light
are crystalline. He cannot escape it,
locate the inner place he has vacated.

No ant on the back of his neck
as he had thought, but sweat starting
to trickle from his hair. Against his ribs,
his arms are numb, one hand tingles.
He is unsure about his legs. Earlier,
sounds turned hazy, stopped.

When he stands and wipes the earth
from his forehead and cheek, light will
slam his other eye, blackbird and wind
sounds and the stream's sloshing
will burst into his ears, and sorely
his legs and arms will rouse back to routine.

Knowing that, he remains longer,
attempting return,
locating sensations and one
by one unhooking them, waiting
for the purity of perfect disconnection.

2. Past

Memory finds a Sunday when
the late afternoon sun continually
dissolves in cloud and reappears
east of one o'clock. He is doing
nothing. On his belly watching
red ants scurry. On his back to see
a hawk disappear in the sun. At
the creek to scoop and drop handfuls
of minnows. Not aware his new
clothes are hand-me-downs. Not
aware he is alone. Not thinking
anything. This is the afternoon
the fox steps from the tall grass,
gazes at him, then prances off.
And the bluegreen dragonflies
helicopter in the bulrushes while
the Vs from two slow muskrats
touch and lazily overlap. All the
trivial sensations sliding down
the sides of memory into this day.
A wheat grass stem sucked white
tasting of wind and heat and dust.
None of it going anywhere. He isn't
going anywhere. The day repeating
itself and the boy becoming a boy
into dazzling blue infinity.

3. Future

His memory purged and
replenished precisely as he wished,
his drift to romantic folly
reduced to a docile urge.

Images and words flow from his eyes
onto bygone screens,
the pages of forgotten books;
lyrics, their coy melodies, spill
from his ears into antique radios–
pillage from the grey museum
that induced replicas of love.
His rue an echo in marble.

He holds his arms to the sky
the way one hoists a child in joy
and feels the lift and peel
of lovers leaving, the cool
thrill of air on his chest,
lips numb, fingers tingling.
The flit of dragonflies in reeds
where blackbirds sing.

A distant heavy door slams
and reverberates in vacancy.
Silence, then, immaculate.

Inside Information

This room is all there is,
this room
with us in it and it moves
with us as we move, our positions
never changing, though our bodies
shrivel closer to the earth.

Those teenagers circling in vehicles
have it right: there is no place to go.
The comic knows: *Have you ever noticed
that wherever you go, there you are?*

There is no back porch to this room.
No outside.

The room will fool us, its wallpaper
inventive, its mutable furnishings,
and though we will dwell here forever,
we will never doubt its small illusions,
such as yesterday, such as death.

Nothing

Nothing waits in your empty car
not reflecting on the mirror
dreaming of wide open spaces
where you will be together always.
Nothing travels light and goes
far on an empty stomach.

Nothing remains in your house
when you leave for work
reading your secret journals
wishing the pages were blank.

Nothing coughs you out of sleep
then leans against a wall
watching you pace the night,
aware you worry about it.

Nothing keeps you from work
with temptations – space, peace,
the open way, parentheses
erased, an expunging void.

Enticing in veil and black crepe,
nothing zeros in on your vacant mind,
breathes, *Embrace me forever.*
But you remember your mother saying
Nothing can harm you, and you resist.
Nothing could have predicted you would.
Nothing crawls into your bed and waits to happen.

Traveller's Advisory
for Robert Kroetsch

Wherever you go others are absent.
You feel the spaces they make
in every foreign landscape.

Some you placate with postcards.
The others, always in mind,
speak at unsuspected times.

Momentum takes you over borders
not shown on the old map
you study at every stop.

The paper thinning into space,
light riddling the cities,
roads, coves, memories.

Where is time taking you this
time? What distance will you make
before the past presents a shape?

No scales, no legends translate
voids to voices, empty reaches
into longed-for faces.

You always know who isn't there
and turn half expectantly
to where someone turning ought to be.

Dark Bodies

There exist in the heavens therefore dark bodies as large as and perhaps as numerous as stars themselves.   *–Pierre de Laplace (1796)*

A darker section of night.
Whole flights of geese, planes, stars
vanish. Astronomers peer in
with instruments and their light

never returns. Lovers do not
know their vision is unrequited,
imagine a moon, its myths
renewing themselves with fire.

Seekers fall in, and those left,
clutching connections gone
slack, fabricate data
to explain their amazement.

Oracles claim revelations,
thrive on the void. Profits
zoom for firms that make
potions to erase black spaces.

While deep in the dense core
of the absence of everything,
you remain still, close, intense
in the vast wrap of gravity.

He Reads from the Persian

Hallaj, the Sufi mystic,
declares *My love and I
are one.* He employs
the metaphor of the moth,
but since his mating flame
is God he has to die.
Obligingly, he is
tortured and crucified,
love's consummation.

And so the good Hallaj
bleeds in rapture.
By contrast, God most
wisely had the first
parents split in pain
from one reed then join
to make two children.

He saw the parents love
those two past restraint
and in tears succumb
to eating them, each a child.

That the race might thrive
God diminished their supply
of love ninety-nine percent,
which for a time sufficed
for all the honest forms.

Till their children devised
filters for the one percent–
deifying half the reed,
fearing the fusion.
Wasting point seven five
on selected excrement.

God they were smart, those
Persians, to see the knife
edge between over and under
loving and to calculate to
the decimal (point two five)
why he's alone again tonight.

Walkman Boy

Rainy days the Walkman Boy leans
in doorways hands jammed in jeans,
his neat machine a pacemaker
in the pocket of his jacket.
Cords looping to each ear
deliver molten doses
that spray inside his head
like wild high-pressure hoses.

Day after day this is what he does,
cindercrete eyes looking
nowhere, arms inert, fingers
and toes not snapping, not
tapping. Mulling gum
while cops and medics
attend the day's mistakes.

His consciousness is complete.
He has new batteries and hits
of Poison and Megadeth.
When the gas line explodes
he does not adjust his set.

* Tabloid * Love *

SHAPE-CHANGING PRESENCE HAUNTS CITY
   3-D specs bring it leaping
   from the daily blur
   apprehensive inarticulate
   wanting in spite of appearances
   its malformations
   to clasp you in its many arms

MANIFESTATION PUZZLES CROWDS
   They cannot turn it on or
   fold it out or peep into it
   no soundtrack no sunset
   no misty scripted repartee
   no place to insert money
   What is it they repeat circling
   like sharks around a sunken chest

MAN GIVES BIRTH TO MYSTERY THING
   Confounding Man who thought
   it could be done without pain
   and even that he'd done it
   the common misconception
   this weak ungainly larval thing
   that gutted him
   and altered everything forever
   with its claims its largesse

GROWTH DEVOURS PILOT
   It's definitely a labour union
   with enough sweat and tears
   to stop an air invasion
   but it happens It happens
   in such small increments
   the clouds surprise you

GHOST SHIP SPOOKS SOUTHERN PORTS
    It moves before them but they
    are like those islanders
    who stood while the Santa Maria
    sailed into their cove and saw
    nothing since they had no map
    nor matrix for large sailing craft

    Back into jungle they turn
    spears raised for prey or rivals
    while the harbour fills with miracles

Play By Play

The carnivores are devouring
their smaller rivals.
Empty seats glisten with blood.
Diehards cluster like tumours
on the bright red rows.

Ice crystals have wrinkled
the holographic cheerleaders.
The artificial turf is slick
with lies beneath dimming
artificial eyes.

The half-time guest was
the old pro Charlie Olson.
After nostalgic footage
he praised the stars, declared
the game is mostly mental.

Good intentions collide with
their guards. The centre cannot hold
onto anything. The rule book
sick with equivocations
is kicked over fallen uprights.

What's this? Something's in the air!
Something taking shape at last!
This could be it! Yes, it looks–
Yes, they're on their feet and
my god look at that! God almighty!

Last Overtime

No one knows the score.

Once there was a ball.
A direction it should go.

On the sidelines a dark figure
points a gun into the sky.

Toward the River
for Henry

No wife, no cops to catch you
squeaking through winter bluster,
the river waiting patient as a postal box,
fish in its ice like stiff phrases,

& knowing it hits you hardest
in January, all the mass solid
down to the earth's eight ball core,
your blood a trickle freezing
on one of the words for snow.

Or it's another rehearsal & you return
tenured to plan tomorrow's classes–
the daily attrition by ignorance,
the daily cowardice by brilliance,
the protective glitter flaming
to ash in the old ash pan.

But no, you've done it. The bridge
receding into clouds, your sleeves
applauding in the uprush breeze,
a grey bundle plummeting,
head cooling at last.
Filling at last
with words.

Occupants

Each decade the nation relocates, blotching mailing lists
and address books, depressing the post office.
Houses empty and refill like tidal pools–
subsidized duplexes, custom-builts with decks and saunas.
Banks and realtors compounding a frenzy of profits
from lives in ebb and flood, the pulse of commerce.

Families appear in their sitcom windows, as if someone
were switching them on and off, a restless thumb on a very remote
control, new lives aligned in neighbourless neighbourhoods.
Troubled couples try new networks, workers move to places
where work must be better, the jaded seek cities to excite them.
The kids on a merry-go-round of playground counterparts,
parents grooming new yards, TV-numbed, dozing, nameless.

A husband dies, a wife escapes, a career withers, the cat is poisoned.
The moving van drops ramps, men in overalls struggle
under mattresses, pianos, refrigerators, precious boxes.
Hedges are planted, fences erected, swing sets come and go.

This searching for the proper ground, this uprooting
and transplanting to occupy what once were fields,
and woods where animals lived their lives entire.

This is how we flee and seek each other. How we mix
and sift the mysteries. These flights into our distances.

Tidal Bores at Truro

An aerosol of fine rain mingles
earth and grass. Brochures give
the precise time, but anxious
for the best view the tourists
cluster early, some in cars,
some outside with umbrellas.
The narrow creek and shy rain
meet unseen in the gorge below.
The woman from Hull who
used to teach geography chirps
to her friend on the causes of tides,
recites stats on the Fundy surge.

A car coughs, sprouts headlights
feeble and diffuse, wipers teasing
the glass. Suddenly two lamps
blare into the gorge churning rain.
People press to the verge and see
no miracle, just a lone heron
poised and solemn in the creek.
The woman from Hull falls silent.
One by one their fingers target him
brilliant white against brown cliffs
where rain now climbs the cones of light.

It is all they have to watch, this single
channel making them a nation
in the night. After a long hush,
his head turns slowly and he takes
one smooth stride toward the far bank.
Another stride and he's on shore.
Then a far-off roar and a snout
of water with a brow of foam rushes
up the creek like a jealous lover.

Mysteries of Everyday Life

1.

Inside the library's *On Becoming
a Novelist* by John Gardner I find
a crinkled black and white photo–
a thin-legged blonde in panties
and chemise smiling delectably
while holding an open umbrella
behind an unstrapped shoulder.

Did she make it as a novelist, or
did her lover, the one who so
casually left her in the section
about the personal sacrifices
of writers? Did Susan Swan or
Robert Kroestch have this book
before me? The librarian says
they don't keep such records.

2.

Memos from "King" on the Co-op
bulletin board. Tacked amidst
auction notices, misspelled ads
for hardly-used bicycles, like-new
waterbeds: *I'm still waiting* printed
above his name in quotations. A wit
once scrawled *What for asshole?*
underneath one of these.

My last encounter with any King
was a friend's long-tongued dog.
He would prance after whoever
spoke to him until he was chased
home. I have a vision of this
Irish setter in sunglasses, long
curved tail jutting through
his trench coat flap, striding in
on hind legs, and posting the note.
Maybe he wants to let survivors
of the old neighbourhood know
he's ready to romp once more.

3.

On my doctor's door, perhaps eight
inches from the floor a mouth
floats on the glossy varnish,
a perfect scarlet kiss, the kind
that used to make me ache
when left in the bathroom by
someone's girlfriend, pressed soft
on Kleenex or glossy on the mirror.

Was my doctor up to some down
and dirty on-the-floor grappling
with a very near-sighted blonde
in panties, chemise and umbrella?
Or was it the door-maker's woman,
after months of neglect, leaving
a souvenir kiss with his real love
positioned over sawhorses?

4.

The way parts of our lives break
off and drift into other lives.
Our most painful intimate
moments theirs to lift to their
lips like a kiss on Kleenex.

IV

River of Light

The most beautiful thing in the world is, of course, the world itself.

–Wallace Stevens

Casey Quinn's Beatitudes

Certain as pre-dawn air is sweet
and sedate just waiting for a breeze
at the lower lake in May, it's there.
Or when the months are three-
and four-syllabled so they can bear
hushed carols of snow-pure birth.
And when dusk smoulders down
it's there. Whether in dank
or thirsty air, in pinewood glens
or the scrawl of wind on shoals.
Even on the raven's open wing
gleaming vermilion, plum
and jade in the squint of sun.
Fresh as the smack of spring
on the cheek of stale March days,
it's there, to be sure. And not in your
fine briefcase, lad.

                And so partake.
Crush darkness and ignite a screen
of peacock, cardinal and canary
fireworks that expire like sparks
in your lap, trajectories perfect
as well-packed buttocks. Why talk of
your "secured retirement savings"
with this dazzle in your middle?

Soak yourself in succulent oils
till your skin opens and craves
kisses, the exquisite carpet-crush
under supple foot, the crisp nip
of linen sheets, the singe
of skin, lips that render all
your flesh tender as nipples.

                    Your breath,
the sibilant rush of it in moist
pink passages, your body filling
with it like a lover receiving
love, the familiar miracle
of its lust for oxygen, the zing
of its leap from pulse to revel in cells.
Great god what glorious beasts
we be. What peaks we sing from
and sure enough yes descend aching,
spent, ready to savour repose.

                    Music,
art, books and food that burst
on us, in us like lunatic seeds,
their increase teasing modesty
to recreate their first embrace.
The luscious dishes we devise,
the lure of them, fragrances
that quicken or soothe. Ah, these
sweet comrades of solitude.

Goggle now at this canvas while
the first allegro from *Le quattro*
stagione sparkles: A Glendalough
stream all mossy stones and silver
flow before dusky trees. That vague
sunglow smudge on tilting clouds–
such natural accord, great god.
That artist, the famed Anonymous,
and Vivaldi lilt in concert,
both dead long ago and stowed
like brutes in peasant graves.

And where was time with its lists
and missions all that while
we gazed and listened there agog?
Out of mind. Mind, too, its play
and passions, the way just then
I mentioned the pauper burials.
How I wonder did those primates
ever come to think up thinking?

Memory and sorrow, too, the flit
of thoughts, their melding
into restless swarms – dream,
reverie, vision, fancy – like small
rainforest birds every tone and tinge
darting on amethyst, indigo,
ruby lines that never tangle.
Reason weaving designs, riddling,
clutching its crown, resolving
snags, inspecting calendars
so the griping bills get eased.

Or into the droop of hammock
letting the old head's bric-a-brac
surface randomly, or sensations
shrill their razzmatazz.
But cleansed of fuss and hum–
a lone leaf on the brow of summer
in a pond. Isn't it so, the mind,
bliss master, captain of cages?
It's true, I love my brain more
than chocolate or Kerry's brew.

In winter when the sun shouts
flat and hot through that big front
window, I strip me down naked
to thrill the widow across the way
and stretch out and bask in it
with my dog Bock. And so we wag
away many a warm afternoon
reading, sleeping, scratching.

Ah, legs, of course. How they look
and work, what a blessing
they are, legs. A symphony
is walking, such harmonies
of muscles, tendons, ligaments,
the architecture of foot–
toes, arch, heel, the physics
of knees and hips moving me
on these levers to my lover's
lips or off to fetch with Bock.
I like to be at pools or beaches
where I can gaze at legs unclad.
It's near to watching a child
asleep all nuzzled in a basket,
or the fish-scale sky at dusk
off Dunmanus Bay in Cork.

Bram and Ria come by, or I'm
to them, or we're to Kerry's
for a pint and sometimes the talk
zings along so tangy, it's sad
I am to leave and wring the snake.
It's art the way we waltz a point,
together but opposite, sure to rebut
whatever's voiced just to tease
ourselves from the slug of custom.
And being out or in with them
or the others is great god a wonder.
And being alone before or after,
with Bock gone to panic cats,
is as well a wonder.

                    Partake, then.
Or amass money, polish your spoils,
go pump your pickle and despair.
There's too much common miracle
to waste it glazed and puggled.
Fill each instant over-brim. Let
spill its perils. Look, I lick them yet.

Sandhill Cranes Near Last Mountain Lake

Clear morning sweet with wild mint and
blue-eyed grass. The sedge-spiked marsh,
hemmed with bulrushes and cattails, twining
between slopes and spreading flat and gold
as a pounded coin in the distant stillness.

Muted trumpet notes, from the south
where a speck hoves into sight, becomes
a crane with wide-waving wings, head forward
on a slender neck. Then another crane and
another and more fill the air. Their notes
grow hoarse and tinny and are echoed
louder, clearer down the line of stately
dipping wings. They sweep over a hilltop,
then with great walloping strokes, swoop,
land with a few running strides, and settle
near the crest, regal, tall as grown wheat.

Slate grey feathers overwashed with rust,
an inset carmine patch from crown to beak,
eyes alert and bright as amber agates.
Stepping stiff-legged with a tiny pause
before each foot lifts and drops lightly,
bustle feathers shaking with each step.

Silence while long necks curve and search
the earth with sinuous grace. Now and then
one rises to scan the hills or a head
swerves to where an insect scarpers.
Slowly they forage toward the hilltop.
One periscopes the scene beyond.
Then they strut over and are gone,
except for two that linger in the sun.

One approaches the other solemnly
bowing   bobbing   gesturing with
half-closed wings
then hops on dark stilts
over the other's head
long legs
jutting stiffly   wings aflicker
as if swatting gnats.

The other joins an intricate jig
of angle-winged struts
                                    zany whirls
flutters
                    glides
                            gambols.

They skip and flap in half-circles,
vault as high as cannon-shot clowns,
legs straight out, black bills skyward.
They jump and arch their necks, jack-
knifing between open wings.

As the dervish speed increases they
croak and cackle like delirious crows.

Suddenly in mid-gyration they freeze.

One swaggers forward,
bends, grasps a twig in its bill,
and with a quick snap of the neck,
flings it down the slope.

Then they stroll together over the hill.

Prairie/Fire
for Leith Knight

Fire loves prairie – wild grass
immensities withered by sun,
wind to give it wings, white rocks
to smudge, huge sky to smear with smoke.

And after, white bones on black tracts–
the dreams of demons.

Cree hunters caught the breeze,
breathed embers into a wide blaze
and stampeded buffalo to cliffs.

The Earl of Southesk, authentic British
twit, stoked his meerschaum
and, ignoring dry ground everywhere,
tossed the match over his shoulder.
The conflagration blurred two sunsets.

Then steam and metal wheels,
      hot boxes and threshers,
            stubble, smudge and straw stack blazes–
                to prove man's fire works.

Thousands of square miles charred.
Cattle, crops, homes consumed
by flames faster than a runaway team,
a rumble like a summer storm, leaving
black wastes from lake to lake.

But the stubborn returned and rebuilt,
and the land recovered
with a deeper, sweeter greenness.

The River of Light

Ice crystals the forecaster promised
between plugs for Pepsi and Dristan
are a beam of needles in the sun
moving clean from west to east
around trees, poles, people,
trembling silver in the breeze.

They tingle on my face like some
hallowed gaze. My creased eyes
squeeze and water from their graze.
What more is there to standing deep
in grace, where light in light
lifts you out and into space?

Sweet weeping – how else to greet
splendour on your street? And I
in the driveway one mitt to my
cheek, one on the shovel, feel
inside the ecstasy, outside myself,
on earth and in the radiance.

A high, hypnotic cadence hovers
on the slightly wavering stream
releasing me, holding me,
as if a star burst down the street
and the sound became the gleam
that makes this brilliant rush.

The grate of shovel on concrete
draws me from the drifting sheen,
restores me to my aching back.
Grounded again, I hoist and heave
the nuisance snow neglecting
how it shimmers as it falls.

Rehearsals

This blindness could be foreseen.
He was mad for the feel of things–
the sleek sheen of porcelain,
the brittle crystal of crusted snow,
inner thighs, their silken skin.
Eyes closed always.

In the cellar he'd file his fingers,
skin dusting to the earthen floor.
Slide hands alive in the gloom
along the shelves of preserves,
the broom, the shovel, cool
jagged fragments of coal.

Each room a song. Bath-soft fingers
along the bristles of a brush,
the lushness of towels, the shiver
of chrome fixtures. Eyes closed
for focus, naming each sensation,
rehearsing absence.

Today hearing Peterson play
he sees hands on the keyboard,
feels the moonlight of the keys,
the rough edges of furious riffs.
This blindness a room of blooming hands,
touching, retouching, subtle as leaves.

Song of Your Skin

for Sharon

Beneath my skin your skin
pebbles, puckers, ripples
and O the sensation
knowing you pulse within,

that my breath's enough
to summon your throat's blush,
that you hear the words I
sign with an eyelash on your thigh.

I can never see, never feel
enough of you – the moles, the mounds
that hold my bites,
the hollows, the fleshy rounds

that dimple
with the notion of a finger,
and that I cannot kiss without
a tremor.

My lips and tongue go mad
trying to take in
the lyric rise and fall,
the song of your skin.

Midnight Skater

It is night and it means
nothing to have come alone
to this outdoor rink
to skate. The mongrel who
hardly slows to lift his leg
to the gate knows that.
But I am breathing in
the clean slice and scrape
of blades with the bite of cold
air deep into my chest.
And I rekindle to
the heft of the stick,
the click of the puck
cupped backhand to fore,
the smack and thunder
of the boards booming off
the slumbering houses.
The moonlight on the ice
is as clean as grace.
Speeding from the dark
I skate along its sheen
right into the sky.

"Colourless Green Ideas Sleep Furiously"

Cells and cells of concepts spurned
as infantile or trite seethe in their sleep.
One feeble green idea dreams of fame–
robust and waving to zealous throngs
from the back of a two-block limousine.
He wants his season on banners and bumpers.
He wants to mate, mutate and sizzle in the lobes
of intellectuals and idiots. He wants to be
the indelible slogan everyone hums.

Drab! How dare those snobs call him drab–
those ugly linguistic paleontologists,
those semi-detached existentialists,
those fading Fabians in lumpy cardigans.

In his latest dreams, he stockpiles arms
and lingers in gangliatic slums,
mingling with gangster notions and snarling
for revolution. Even though his mother
warned: "Always watch your syntax," he now
cohabitates with hyperboles and loose
analogies in Noam Chomsky's brain.

The Abdication of Winter

Winter did not want to be winter
any longer, sulked through November
munching days in the back of its jaw
absentmindedly, an exiled monarch
scowling at the loyal retainers
who stomped and shivered encouragement.
"To hell with cold and frost-scrawled windows.
Let machines snow the slopes for skis
and sleighs, and ice the sheets for skates.
Let them spray the fields with Dream Whip.
Let the bears lie down and rise unsnoozed
and shamble confused into campsites."

December resembled September. Children
went scarfless at recess and rollicked
in parks. When the delegations arrived,
Winter buttoned its great white coat,
turned its back and slumbered on a glacier.
Owners of resorts and tow truck fleets,
snow plow operators and parka makers wept,
but Winter never weakened. Thousands
of Canadian weather wimps vacillated
at the forty-ninth parallel unsure if they
should dare to be unafraid, unsure if
Winter wasn't waiting until the exchange
rate soared even higher. But Christmas
was dreary beige and brown and people
barbecued turkeys, rode bicycles to church.

Before long, horn-rimmed weathermen
were stars on talk shows with maps
of ocean currents, satellite shots of
holes in the sky and legends of *El Niño*.
A professional environmental doomster
radiantly predicted the end of Miami
and other such coastal afflictions.
A cult of positive thinkers in Moose Jaw
organized a weekend of ersatz coughing
and sneezing, but Winter declined to be
impressed. Deconstructionists put forth
a new "wintertextuality" to "recast
the specious winter-summer binary."
A feminist wrote an article on Winter's
gender and consequent motivation.

Winter, in time, grew bored with
not being winter, so when the cute child
arrived in synthetic furs and recited
a cute poem cutely, it twirled off
a few desultory blizzards. Even though
Winter knew the cute child was from
an agency and the poem composed by
a committee of advertising men. For this
mistake Winter endured a scourge of
cute children cutely reciting cute poems.
So Winter whistled over some wolves
from the Shield and the moppets stopped.

With March Winter began to chuckle.
That dainty-toed kibitzing Spring
wouldn't have much of an entrance
after this warm-up act. It even
rumbled out a rainstorm to pillage
some of Summer's thunder. April
was as ho-hum as Winter had hoped.
By then Winter was eager to go south.
Hot damn thought Winter *those down
unders won't know what never hit them.*

Throats of Stone

Great archaeologists, like great artists, have curious minds and intense imaginations.
                                                          –Richard Leakey

To note what isn't there. To arrange
creatures in air the way once they
might have been and dream a tree
to hold them. One so real colleagues
calibrate its limbs. The best scientists
are poets who draw with metaphors.
Such as Salomon Reinach's leap
from the modern hunting totems of
Australian aboriginals to the cave
drawings of paleolithic people.

Hunting magic seemed a good theory,
and many archaeologists enjoyed
its shade. André Leroi-Gourhan
could not. He wondered why the beasts
on the walls were not the ones whose
bones fringed the ancient fire sites.
Why draw entrees not on the menu?
Maybe, thought Leroi-Gourhan, we have
discovered art and not a shopping list.
Caves of passions, visions, fictions.

He saw certain animals always put
in the same places in repeated patterns:
deer at entrances; oxen, horse, bison
in main chambers; tigers and panthers
snarling in the deep and narrow dark.
Other scientists concurred until sex
entered the pictures: Leroi-Gourhan
declared some images were male;
others, female. Gender wars ensued
and chainsawed the budding proposition.

Lately near Ariège two archaeologists
have been singing in the caves.
From tapes of their three octave span,
they drew graphs and maps of their music
and found the animal images massed
in places of highest resonance. Perhaps
shamans used these places to praise
and curse, echoes of shaking syllables
astonishing the select, spilling from mouth
of rock to sky. The earth in ecstasy.

In the flicker of voice and lamp light
off damp walls, and black clutches
of demons twitching left and right, tigers
may have prowled; panthers, lunged.
While glacial gusts howled above,
artists sang and made signs for music
in the long stone throats. Said here
is magic, here our drums and whistles,
our voices will shake into meaning, will
reveal who sings these beasts and why.

Empty Holsters

for my creative writing students
at the Outlaw Ranch, Custer, South Dakota

You heft the stuff of lies,
ransom notes, death decrees.
Whistling, you flip grenades
onto the innocent page. Moves
that would get you captured
and killed in countries where pens
are automatic weapons and poems
contraband. Places where the police
are students of poetry and soldier-
critics butt cigars in writers' eyes.

In this land, other dangers. Posses
track computer-chip toys
and hucksters' lies are more
potent than poems. Here we look
grim on Not Wanted posters. Still
we ransom poems with time.
Because we have no choice.
Because silence knocks on the door.

Meditation on Two Doves
for Lorna Crozier

Two grey-stemmed doves on a grey roof
in grey dawn, legs invisible, bob
on air above asphalt shingles.
How we know the absent is present.

The way we once assembled nights
from the pulse of darkness,
the sweet breath of wheat
thick with frog and cricket clamour,
the pelt of moths on dusty screens,
the muffled whir of nighthawks' wings–
the feast of minding these invisibles.

Thus the swells and scars of lovers'
bodies are in your lines, but never
your body – its small singing mouths,
its sprinkle of freckles like flung grain,
its sleek preen to water's perfect
hand, the white moon ripple
where the scalpel nipped, the tangle
swirl and flow of spilling hair,
hollows filled with whispers,
pale drifts of lips upon your breasts.

Somewhere out of sight you sense
the tremor in your body
and translate that stammer
into the songs of birds
that dance on us with unseen legs.

Valencia Poems

Trees feel the piccolo
riffs of dawn,
the day's ardor of
golden songs,

how evening slurs and
stretches notes,
sun a trumpet's glint
in dusky smoke,

and believe they can
compose on air,
translate passion
into lyric repertoire.

Look at this grove's
luscious glossolalia,
its incredible
orange babble!

V

Recitin from a Feelin

I believe
> *I believe my time ain't long*
I believe
> *I believe my time ain't long*
>> –Robert Johnson

Recitin from a Feelin: Robert Johnson's Blues

1.

Stackhouse Houston

You think you ain't heard Robert's music
but you has providin you heard the likes
of Chuck Berry, Eric Clapton, the Stones
an' hundreds others been skinnin his chops.

That boy packs blues with so much muscle
they punch you whap in the chest till your heart
pains. His fingers so agile an' supple,
Keith Richards thinks it's two dudes pickin.

Some folks say he'd trek out to a midnight
crossroads an' meet with Satan who'd tune
that scratch-up guitar an' teach him licks
wilder'n any mother-born man could ever hatch.

In seven years Robert pretty well laid down
all the trails musicians been ramblin since.
You ain't heard Robert Johnson, man you ain't
heard where rock n' roll got delivered its soul.

2.

Carrie Spencer, His Half-Sister

How it was I guess I don't mind tellin:
my mama, she be Mrs. Spencer, but she
had a mischief with one Noah Johnson
and Robert be the consequence.

First mama take me and Robert round
workin the camps. Then back to my daddy
and his new woman Serena where I stay
but Robert at seven be too many handsful.

By then mama married to Dusty Willis
in Robinsonville so Robert shuffled there.
Mama say he be 15 when she explain him
who his daddy be and how he long time gone.

Right off that boy commences callin hisself
Robert *Johnson* stead o' Spencer, no matter
what folks sez, and the rest o' his life
he keeps his good eye out for that man.

I know how he 'magined one day things
be gleam and glory when they two meet:
Robert be a ticket. Noah from the crowd come
and hug him and tell him good lovin lies.

Near the end whatever place he be stop
he scout him all the jugs and jooks and flops
and always, always he never finds his daddy.

3.

His Step-Father Dusty Willis

Couldn't get that boy one day behind no mule,
nothin for him but cheap music and cheatin school.

R.L. Windum

We'd even play at recess—
harmonica, harp and fake
husky voices hackin through
Howlin Wolf and Kokomo Arnold.
I jus trifled for a time, you understan,
but Robert he studied them blues,
tanned his fingers learnin
Charlie Patton, Whiskey Red, Son House.
Studied Ike Zinnerman
who usedta sit on tombstones
just to get the feel.
Played the courthouse steps
levee camps, road gangs,
any chicken shack would have him.

4.

Ike Zinnerman

Likes to drive me crazy, that boy
wolfin me to teach him this,
teach him that. Moonshine gone,
moon long down and Robert
still beggin one more strum.

Bout then he starts notchin up
a few numbers of his own.
Hive off inna woods alone
with scribble book and guitar,
come out with some upright blues.

Those long orchid fingers
of his flit that board like birds
on hot wires. He could curve notes
and slide the pitch right to Texas.

Willie Brown

Got so Robert could play any music.
Heard him do "My Blue Heaven"
and "Tumblin Tumbleweeds,"
seen him do square dances,
polkas, hillbilly. Hear it once,
Robert have it. Bunch of us
be conversin, radio in next room
playin some new Leroy Carr item,
Robert keep right talkin with us.
That night, do that Carr song
dead smack. I swear he have
four brains hooked to four hands.

5.

Carrie Spencer

After his wife and his baby die
no denyin he like the henhouse life
though I think he was mostly true
to Callie 'fore she broke down sick.

When he with Stella Lockwood,
Lord, she good to him and he
good to her. Teach her boy Robert
all his secret playin strategies.

See, those guitar slants he hatch
he not passin round like ribs.
Someone be studyin his hands
Robert break the song and be gone.

Got so he growed too neglectful whose
fire he be keepin stoked, y' understan.
When your songs excite the women
their men can put on nasty ways.

6.

Honeyboy Edwards

Weren't too many Delta women never heard of Robert.
What he'd do soons we'd hit Tchula, Walls, Beulah,
Midnight, Lamont, some such place, Robert'd scout him
the homeliest witch in town, spread some honey on her.
Have himself a sugar nest anytime he want.

Corrie Craft

I'da gone with him myself, Callie hadn't,
so dapper an' so sad. She say
his fingers so roughed from strummin
he soak his feet soft in oils
and excite her skin with them.

He come honest to the blues–
his share of leavin an' bein' left,
wife, baby dead, his natural father
stayin disappeared all his life.
Most to killed his heart
that. An' leavin Callie and the kids.

That guitar makin shadows
to his voice while it slur an' moan,
sweet-talkin like some lonely soul
so beautiful high on pain.

7.

Carrie Spencer

Born: May 8th, 1911.
Dead: August 16th, 1938.
Just a few quick years
to make such fame
and yards of rumours
how his last set end.

Corrie Craft

Shot dead from a Midnight woman
he done two-timed once too much.

Malted Milk Jackson

This pair hootched-up gandy dancers gets
fightin over a woman Robert's marked out.
Fore you could spit Robert's stuck twice real bad.
They gets away an' likely that juicer who killed
the best blues ever, died rottin of ol' age.

Rev. Tooley Rivers

Counterfeit, all them other lies,
musta bin other folks got planted,
cause I seen him go two year later
in Kansas city at the Blue Match.

He was playin the same devil blues–
booze and sinful easy women–
when he was snatched right off his stool
by the flamin hand of Satan hisself.

8.

Stackhouse Houston

The way I gathered it is that Saturday night
in Greenwood Robert has too many eyes all over
the house man's wife and there was talk she and him
was patchin' down all week. And so durin' a break
some fellas offer Robert a half-pint with a broken seal
and he puts away most of it before he goes back on.

First he's too pained to sing but the crowd wants more
so he tries and plays sick awhile and then collapses.
It was the house man dosed that drink with strychnine, you see,
and it took Robert to pneumonia and that's what took him off.

Honeyboy Edwards

Jimson juice in that jug
was what it truly was
and they slung him to town
and I don't know why
they kept him in a shack
without no doctor
and he was snappin and growlin
three entire days
before he leave the stage for good.

9.

Carrie Spencer

My mama who was Robert's mama she
never told me my little brother was dead.
Said it was to spare me grief.
County buried him in a two dollar box
in Morgan City, Mississippi.
His Daddy's name on the death certificate,
all he ever got from that man,
markin him a bastard,
my little brother.

Mama say that day
the sky was unnatural
still. Like them roadhouse crowds
when almost in blood
he finished singin.

10.

Johnny Shines

First time I heard him play I had to play like that.
One time Calvin Frazier had killed a couple fellahs,
so he team with Robert and me jookin up Highway 51–
St. Louis, Decatur, Chicago, even inta Canada.
He loved to move that man almost more than music.

I'd work on Robert's shifts but it was like a snake
tryin to ride a bicycle. He did these diminished
sixths and sevenths, these walk-on-water riffs, even was
plannin to mix in piano, bass and drums. Who knows
what music that boy mighta made he'da lived to thirty.

For sure Robert's hands playin some of today's music.
He had more licks than a stump fulla puppies. Hell
he made sounds still ain't come outa no 'lectric box.
No Robert, and today's music be back there somewhere else.

This here time some one o' the reglars in Detroit asks
Robert play that crusher he played a few nights back,
laid the joint flat, downright through your forehead sad.
And Robert says, "It's gone. I was jus' recitin from a feelin."

Acknowledgements

The anonymous Chinese song at the start of section one and the quotation from Lao-tzu are adapted from a translation in *The Tao of Tai Chi Chuan: Way to Rejuvenation* by Jou Tsung Hwa.

"A Winter Already Past" and "White Crane Smiling" are based on Japanese tales from *The Mystery of Things* by Patrik Le Nestour.

"Recitin from a Feelin: Robert Johnson's Blues" was inspired by "Love in Vain," a three-part CBC radio documentary written and narrated by David Rea and broadcast in May of 1991. The writer is grateful to Stephen C. LaVere whose accompanying notes for *Robert Johnson: The Complete Recordings* were valuable sources. Other information and inspiration came from Peter Guralnick's *Searching for Robert Johnson*.

"Throats of Stone" is based on a portion of Richard Leakey's *The Origin of Humankind*, 1994.

"The River of Light" derives from "I saw a light that was a river flowing" in *The Divine Comedy, Paradiso*, Canto XXX, 61.

"Prairie Fire" is based on an "Historically Speaking" column by Leith Knight in the *Moose Jaw Times-Herald*.

"Colourless Green Ideas Sleep Furiously" is a sentence composed by linguist Noam Chomsky to illustrate that sense is more than a function of correct grammar and syntax.

An earlier version of this manuscript won the Saskatchewan Writers Guild Poetry manuscript Award in 1995, for which the author thanks the Saskatchewan Writers Guild.

Some of these poems have appeared in the following magazines: *Canadian Author and Bookman, Grain, NeWest Review, New Quarterly, Prairie Fire, Prism, Wascana Review,* and several have been broadcast on CBC radio. Some poems appeared in the Anthologies: *Our Fathers* (Rowan Books), *Vintage 93* and *Vintage 95* (Quarry Press), and *That Sign of Perfection* (Black Moss Press). *Tabloid Love* was featured in the performance piece of that title produced by The Poets Combine.

Gary Hyland left teaching in 1994 to pursue his writing full-time. Born and raised in Moose Jaw, Saskatchewan, Hyland taught high school English there after attending the University of Saskatchewan. He was named a poet laureate of Moose Jaw in 1991.

Hyland has published three poetry collections – *After Atlantis* (1991), *Street of Dreams* (1984), and *Just Off Main* (1982) – and two chapbooks. His work has also appeared in numerous anthologies including *200 % Cracked Wheat, The Writer's Solution, Literature of the Americas, Open Windows,* and *The New Canadian Poets,* as well as in such literary periodicals as *Grain, Quarry, Fiddelhead, Canadian Forum,* and *Capilano Review.* He was also the co-editor of four anthologies – *A Sudden Radiance, 100% Cracked Wheat, 200% Cracked Wheat,* and *Number One Northern.*

Hyland has won numerous awards for his writing and his teaching. A founding member of Thunder Creek Co-operative and Sage Hill Writing Experience, he is also a member of International PEN, the Sage Hill Experience board of directors, has served on the executive of the Saskatchewan Writers Guild, and taught creative writing at the Saskatchewan Summer School of the Arts.

Hyland is a sessional lecturer for the University of Regina. He has three sons and makes his home in Moose Jaw, Saskatchewan.

Born in Australia in 1955, **Miranda Jones** emigrated to Canada in 1980. She eventually settled in Saskatoon, where she received an M.F.A. from the University of Saskatchewan in 1989.

Jones's paintings have been been featured in numerous solo and group exhibitions and appear in a vast array of private and institutional collections. Miranda Jones lives in Saskatoon, Saskatchewan.